Tony Orman
Sea Fishing
from Rock, Beach, Estuary and Boat

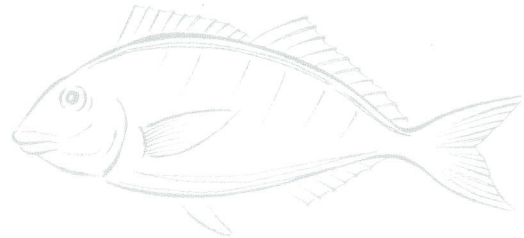

Published by Hyndman Publishing, PO Box 19, Amberley 8251 • ISBN 1-877168-79-3
TEXT: © Tony Orman • DESIGN & ARTWORK: Dileva Design Limted
PRINTING: Spectrum Print

All rights reserved. No part of this publication is to be produced, stored in a retrieval system, or transmitted in any form or by means electronic, mechanical, or photocopying without prior written permission of the publisher.

Contents

- 5 Introduction
- 6 Your Attitude to Fishing
- 8 Common Sea Fish Species
- 14 Sea Fishing Equipment – Tackle, Knots & Rigs
- 21 Targeting the Species
- 26 Common Species Targeting Guide
- 34 Fishing the Estuary
- 36 Surfcasting
- 39 Fishing from Rocks
- 42 Small Boat Fishing
- 48 Lure Fishing
- 53 Saltwater Fly-fishing
- 56 Keeping a Diary
- 59 The Last Cast – Conservation
- 60 Recommended Reading
- 62 Glossary
- 64 How to Fillet a Fish

INTRODUCTION –
The Challenge of Sea Fishing

Saltwater fishing has occurred since the early settlement of both Maori and Europeans in New Zealand. Captain Cook caught snapper at Ship Cove in the Marlborough Sounds in 1769, and in 1642 Dutch explorer Abel Tasman no doubt took the opportunity to fish for sport, and, importantly, fresh food to eat. Just as these early explorers enjoyed sea fishing, so do more than one million of today's New Zealanders, making it the most popular participant sport in the country.

Sea fishers come in many forms – big game fishermen, surfcasters, boaties, youngsters fishing from the jetty or wharf, underwater spear fishers, whitebaiters, and saltwater fly anglers. Fishing in saltwater has almost infinite possibilities, simply because of the varied species of fish off New Zealand's coasts. Methods may range from the traditional handline to sophisticated carbon fibre rods and to the new wave of saltwater fly-fishing. Anyone in New Zealand, male or female, young or old, rich or poor, can take part; it is their traditional right to go fishing for fun and food.

It is beyond the scope of this book to cover everything in the saltwater fishing field, but there are recommendations for further reading and a suggested list of complementary books at the back. This book focuses on the main species available to the shore or boat angler, while making the sea fisher aware of the challenge of exploring and targeting individual species.

Take up the challenge but use the resource wisely – limit your kill by taking just enough for your immediate needs, and do not waste the fruits of the sea.

◀ *Snapper, like this beauty from the Marlborough Sounds, are great fighters.*

Your Attitude to Fishing

Fishing is first and foremost a sport and so should be fun and relaxing. Fishing books rarely devote any pages to the importance of the human factor, yet to handle the equipment well and employ various fishing methods, attitudes are vital. Statistics suggest that only ten percent of anglers catch ninety percent of all fish caught. Why is this? Is it the gear? Quality tackle can help greatly but it's only one factor – buying the top tackle won't immediately transform each and every angler into one of that ten percent elite group.

Many anglers never fulfil their potential because of a tendency to become too set in their ways. As G.E.M. Skues, legendary British trout angler and writer, noted in one of his books, 'The true function of an authority (a writer) is to stimulate, not to paralyse original thinking.' I believe that the key to success in fishing is attitude.

The following are some attitude tips I have picked up over the years:
- Analyse and plan your approach carefully.
- Use good techniques and tactics, but also be open-minded, flexible and adaptable. Anglers can become too dogmatic, swearing by this method or that lure. Try to avoid this close-minded approach.
- Understand that inevitably there will be blank days. Learn to appreciate that no day spent fishing is a failure. Good anglers never assume that they will always make a catch. When they do experience a blank day, it is regarded as a learning experience or a problem to be solved. The more fishing you do, the more you realise you never stop learning.

▲ *A big hump-backed snapper.*

YOUR ATTITUDE TO FISHING

- Fish each and every cast with care and concentration.
- Try to keep your fishing simple and practical. Often the winning formula is based on the simple logic staring you in the face.
- Cultivate a sense of humour in your fishing – encourage yourself to laugh and smile about fishing events. Some anglers are so deadly serious that fishing loses its fun.
- Attitude is also important in making you a good fishing companion. I dislike competitive attitudes between anglers – it detracts from the fishing. If you fish with a friend, do not compare tallies of fish. It is better to say, 'We got four snapper' rather than 'I got three and he only got one.'
- Fish for fun, not to kill. Practise catch and release, and limit the number of fish you take.
- When you are on your own, practise this sporting ethic by American conservationist Aldo Leopold from the book *The Sand County Almanac*: 'A peculiar virtue in wildlife ethics is that the hunter ordinarily has no gallery to applaud or disapprove of his conduct. Whatever his acts, they are dictated by his own conscience, rather than a mob of onlookers. It is difficult to exaggerate the importance of this fact.' This can apply to all fisher folk too.

Enjoy the sport. The author battles a small kingfish on light spinning tackle.

By going sea fishing you are taking part in a life-long sport that is fun and good for you. It is great therapy, arguably adding to your life by the way it dissolves stresses and tensions. Often the biggest highlight, however, is dining on your catch. Enjoy it all!

Common Sea Fish *Species*

BARRACOUTA

These fish are a nuisance as they will swoop in and grab a hooked blue cod, carving up the hapless fish and often breaking off with hook, line and sinker. They make reasonable bait, but are seldom eaten because they are full of bones!

BLUE COD

Delicious to eat, the blue cod is widespread throughout New Zealand, but most abundant around and south of Cook Strait. It is inclined to be a voracious and unselective feeder, eating shellfish, crabs, shrimps, and other small fish.

FLOUNDER

Flounder are found on sandy stretches and in estuaries, and it is in the latter that they are most convenient for the rod and line fisherman. Tackle should be light, preferably a trout fishing style spinning outfit, and with a tiny hook (size 12) baited with a small piece of shellfish such as mussel, or a garden worm and a few split shot for weight.

GARFISH

A miniature swordfish common around estuaries, wharves and rocky shores, garfish are great fighters on ultra-light spinning gear, using a quill float, a size 12 hook and a tiny piece of fish bait. They make excellent eating and are also one of the best snapper baits. If you use dead garfish for snapper bait, a kingfish could strike, so be aware.

Gurnard, which are delicious to eat, are usually caught in sandy areas.

COMMON SEA FISH SPECIES

GROPER
A deep-water fish living around reefs, groper can grow to well over 44kg (100 lbs) but are generally 15–25kg. Often taken on setlines, groper nevertheless can be caught on heavy rod and reel tackle, and saltwater fly-fishing guru Sam Mossman has even caught groper on a fly rod! Groper are top food.

GURNARD
The gurnard is a colourful fish that inhabits mainly sandy areas in both the North and South Islands, but is more abundant north of Banks Peninsula. It feeds on crabs, shrimps, and small fish, and is good to eat.

JOHN DORY
John dory are mainly found around the North Island but are also found as far south as Cook Strait. They like to hang around wharves. A top eating fish, john dory is taken on moving bait – either a live bait or a jig. Soft, plastic, wiggly lures with a lead head are ideal.

KAHAWAI
Once considered to be an unappealing fish that was only good for bait, the kahawai is now regarded as a top sports fish because of its spectacular fighting ability. It usually feeds on baitfish such as yellow-eyed mullet, krill, pilchards and similar species. The kahawai is widespread around both the North and South Islands but more abundant in the North. It can be taken on bait, or provides great sport on light spinning tackle or saltwater fly gear. This species

Groper are often found around deep underwater reefs.

COMMON SEA FISH SPECIES

▲ *Kahawai is now recognised as a premium sporting fish.*

makes reasonable eating if cooked immediately after catching, and is also quite delicious when freshly hot smoked.

KINGFISH

Abundant particularly in the upper North Island, the kingie can move through a variety of habitats from estuaries to reefs, and up to 150 metres deep or more. It is a large, powerful fish that can grow to more than 45kg. Kingfish feed on other fish such as school kahawai and trevally, but will take squid, crabs and large shrimps too. This species can be caught on live bait or by jigging or trolling a lure. Kingfish are good dining.

MOKI

Moki inhabit coastal waters of both the North and South Islands but are more abundant south of Cook Strait. They usually feed in shallow water, close to rocky areas inhabited by kelp. Moki are rarely taken on fish bait but can be caught on shellfish (such as mussels) or crayfish. Heavy in body and growing to over 8kg, moki are powerful fighters, and they are good to eat.

COMMON SEA FISH SPECIES

PARORE

Most common in the warmer North Island waters, parore largely feed on seaweed and sometimes small marine animals. Known in Australia as luderick, they can be caught using sea lettuce or eel grass as bait. Parore need to be gutted immediately on capture, otherwise iodine taints the flesh.

PORAE

This species is more abundant in the North Island, but it can sometimes be found as far south as Cook Strait. Known in Australia as the morwong, the porae eats shellfish, crabs, shrimps, worms and small marine creatures. It is a strong feeder that can provide good sport on light tackle, and is very good eating.

RED COD

Found around both the North and South Islands, the red cod is more abundant south of Cook Strait. Tending to forage over sand and mud bottoms, the red cod feeds on creatures such as crabs and shrimps. This fish has soft flesh.

SNAPPER

Abundant in the North Island and the north of the South Island, snapper also straggle south to Westport on the West Coast, and Kaikoura on the east, but rarely further south. A scavenger and predator of fish, crabs, shrimps and shellfish, snapper roam widely from shallow mudflats in summer

Special techniques are needed to overcome the wariness of the snapper.

COMMON SEA FISH SPECIES

to water up to 100 fathoms deep (182 metres) in winter. A very wary fish that is also unpredictable, snapper will bite well one day but be strangely quiet the next. Snapper can be taken straylining or on a running rig using bait or jigging. Snapper are excellent to eat.

SOLE
Sole are really a subspecies of flounder. They are splendid eating, with delicate white flesh. Distributed throughout New Zealand's coastal waters from 100 metres into close inshore, they are more common in the south. Sole feed on small marine creatures such as worms, brittle stars and sometimes small fish.

TARAKIHI
Of the morwong family, tarakihi are widespread throughout both the North and South Islands but are most abundant south of East Cape. There are two species - the tarakihi and the larger king tarakihi. Usually this fish feeds in shoals and frequents both shallow and deep inshore waters. They feed over rough ground and sandy areas for small crabs, shrimps and shellfish. Top eating.

TREVALLY
The trevally is a strong fighting fish abundant in the north of the North Island but found down to Cook Strait and sometimes further south. It often feeds around reefs and headlands in summer, in surface schools. The trevally is a great fish to jig on light tackle and can be taken on spinning or saltwater fly gear as well as straylining in a berley trail.

HINT:
Trevally have soft mouths so play them carefully. Use a landing net and slip it under the fish before lifting.

TRUMPETER
A strong fighting fish that lives over rocky, often deeper reefs, the trumpeter is occasionally found as far north as the Bay of Plenty, but is more common

COMMON SEA FISH SPECIES

from the Cook Strait south. They are avid feeders and live on squid, octopus and small fish. Trumpeter can grow up to a metre long and about 20kg, but more often are about 50-80cm in length and around 10kg. They are excellent eating.

▼ *Tarakihi are great fighters on light tackle and are succulent to dine on.*

Sea Fishing Equipment –
Tackle, Knots & Rigs

Your equipment should be geared to the fishing you plan to do, and the species you want to target.

RODS

Your rod choice will be determined by the type of fishing you want to do. The first factor to consider is whether you are fishing from shore or boat. For example, in surfcasting, long rods of at least 3.5 metres are used to give the leverage for longer casting and also to keep the line as far as possible above the waves. However, using a surfcasting rod from a boat is not only impractical, due to it's size, but also potentially dangerous to fellow anglers.

Rod design and manufacturing have come a long way in the last 20 years. Today, basically the higher the price, the better the quality. Graphite (carbon fibre) rods are usually superior to fibreglass rods because they are stronger, have more 'beef', and are significantly lighter to carry.

Fishing rods are generally put into three categories – slow, medium and fast. A slow rod is one that bends right to the butt, a medium rod bends to just above the butt, and a fast rod bends only to about a third from the tip. The trend today is towards fast rods.

A hefty blue cod. Cod are voracious feeders and require no special technique.

Generally, rod requirements can be summarised as follows:
- **Surfcasting**: 3.5 metres minimum, fast action.
- **Spinning**: 2 metres or less, medium to fast action.

SEA FISHING EQUIPMENT

- **Jigging**: 2 metres, fast action.
- **Snapper fishing, particularly straylining:** 2 metres, medium action.
- **General boat fishing:** 2 metres or less is preferred. Boat fishing for blue cod does not require specific rod design – a good fibreglass rod about 1.5 to 2 metres long is more than adequate.

I personally like to use the most sensitive rod I can, relative to the species I am hoping to catch. A day I spent fishing at Cable Bay near Nelson illustrates the value of a sensitive rod tip. I had targeted tarakihi, often reasonably bold biters, but not always. On that day I attached an onion bag of ground bait (berley) off the anchor rope and began fishing. Things seemed slow and yet I kept losing the bait. Then I detected just a gentle nod of the sensitive rod tip. I raised the rod and there was a tarakihi. After that I caught a couple of dozen. Two other boats saw me and crowded in. They had the typical boat rod – akin more to a tomato stake or broom stick – and caught nothing, simply because they could not detect the gentle takes on their rods.

> **HINT:**
> Forgot the berley? Perhaps there are mussels on the rocks. Grab a few, crush them on shore and pop in a plastic bag. Drop them sparingly over the side at your fishing spot. It is important not to overfeed fish – just attract them in.

REELS

Saltwater reels are categorised into two types – fixed spool and star drag (free spool) reels. Generally star drag reels are preferred for heavier fish such as kingfish, although there are high-quality fixed spool reels that are capable of handling a good sized kingfish. Both types of reel feature

A fast action rod ties into a snapper. Note bend in top third of rod.

modern technology and quality in the more expensive models – again the more you pay, the better the quality.

One type of fixed spool reel to consider is a 'bait runner.' This is superb for snapper fishing and very adaptable to light tackle fishing for tarakihi, kahawai and other species.

HAND LINE

Let us not forget the humble hand line. I know a few very successful fishermen in the Marlborough Sounds who use a hand line to catch blue cod with great skill and effectiveness. Inexpensive round plastic spools that double as a hand-caster have replaced the old tradition of winding a hand line around a stick or soft drink container.

MONOFILAMENT AND LINES

Monofilament nylon was a revolutionary development in the second half of the 20th century. One advantage was its elasticity, particularly when a long length of nylon was between the angler and the fish. This stretch factor minimised the risk of the nylon breaking. However, elasticity is a disadvantage in detecting a bite and setting the hook. Consequently, the search for a non-stretch fishing line has resulted in a super braid with a stretch factor of zero.

One disadvantage of nylon is its deterioration in sunlight. Ultraviolet light does weaken monofilament. It pays to replace the top section of monofilament each season – perhaps the 100 or 200 metres that has been exposed to sunlight. Another good practice is to store your reel in a dark place when you are not fishing. Alternatively use fluorocarbon nylon, which is said to be resistant to ultraviolet light.

HOOKS

In your tackle box it is a good idea to have a variety of hooks of different sizes. These could range from long shanked cod hooks and beak hooks, to kahl hooks, which are my personal preference for snapper.

SEA FISHING EQUIPMENT

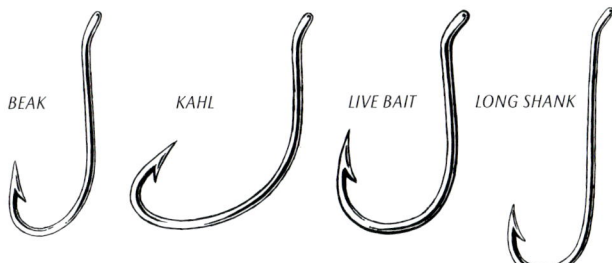

Some hook styles. I personally favour the kahl (sometimes spelt kahle) hook, but long shank is advisable for cod fishing.

SINKERS

Again, a variety are needed. Ball sinkers in varying sizes are usually used on running rigs; pyramid, hollow and spoon sinkers are ideal for surfcasting; dropper and teardrop sinkers are good for boat or wharf fishing for species such as blue cod. A small container of split shot is worth having for catching baitfish.

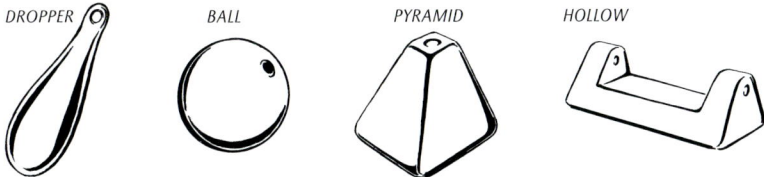

Sinkers – a few styles. Dropper with a ledger rig is ideal for boat fishing for species such as blue cod or tarakihi. The ball sinker is a good one for the running rig, but is not so good if there is a strong wave or current action, as it rolls along the bottom. The pyramid is a good one for surfcasting, as is the hollow style. Other styles are available.

SWIVELS

Swivels have a dual purpose – to stop the line twisting, and to serve as a bottom limit (stopper) for the sinker on a running rig.

OTHER EQUIPMENT

- **Gaff**: A gaff should always be carried for big fish such as kingfish, shark, or stingray. On rocks a long-handled, or better still a telescopic-handled gaff is needed.
- **Net**: Wherever practical, a net is preferable to a gaff. For snapper fishing, a net is indispensable. Again, when fishing from rocks or a high boat, a long or telescopic handle is best.

SEA FISHING EQUIPMENT

- **Tackle box**: You can buy purpose designed tackle boxes, or hardware stores sell toolboxes that serve the purpose admirably.
- **Knives**: It is best to get two, one with a thin blade for filleting fish and the other with a heavier blade for cutting bait.
- **Rod stand**: Whether surfcasting or rock fishing, it is very convenient to have a stand to hold the rod. Metal rod stands can be purchased from tackle stores or a simple one can be made with a metre-high piece of PVC pipe of suitable diameter that is tapered at one end. This end can then be driven into the sand or pushed into a rock crevice.
- **Fishing pliers/hook remover**: A long-handled gadget that is very handy when removing a hook from a sharp-toothed species such as a barracouta or shark.
- **Gimbal belt/harness**: If you are targeting big fish such as kingfish, a gimbal belt is indispensable.
- **Polarised sunglasses**: Every serious angler should have these. They cut glare and reflection from the surface, enabling you to see fish moving down below.
- **Berley container:** These can be bought from your local sports store or made from a PVC tube of large diameter. A bucket with a dozen or so holes bored in the bottom or side will do the job too. Or try an onion mesh bag or one of the plastic mesh bags that holds kiwifruit.
- **Bait-tying elastic cotton**: If you want to use shellfish as bait, such as for moki, tie the soft part of the shellfish on with this. Alternatively an old piece of nylon stocking can be used to enclose the shellfish.

> **HINT:**
> *Some like using a very long trace with a running rig but it can pose problems when landing a fish from a boat. The swivel and sinker hit the rod tip and the 5 metre trace is too long to reach to net the fish! A 2 metre trace is ample.*

▼ *Teamwork and a landing net – both indispensable for boat fishing.*

SEA FISHING EQUIPMENT

- **Live bait bucket**: If you are live baiting for snapper or john dory, a bucket for freshly caught garfish or yellow-eyed mullet is handy.
- **Torch**: This is essential if you are fishing at that magical time of evening into dusk and dark.

RIGS

- Simple Ledger Rig

Simple ledger rig with dropper and two hooks. Ideal cod rig.

- Simple Running Rig – sinker near hook

- Running Rig with Trace

Two running rigs. Top is the sinker right against the hook with no trace. Small sinkers are best with this. Bottom is the running rig with trace (leader) of heavier breaking strain nylon.

- Live Bait Rig

Live bait rigs – through the nose (a) and top of back (b). Putting the hook through by vent (marked X) tends to make the fish swim shallower, i.e. nearer the surface.

Threading a whole baitfish (e.g. pilchard, yellow-eyed mullet) onto a hook. First incision with hook is made near tail; the last is through the eye as shown, then a half hitch around tail.

SEA FISHING EQUIPMENT

KNOTS

These are basic knots for starters. Master these and you'll have a knot for most occasions.

- Simple Loop the Hook Rig – for ledger rig

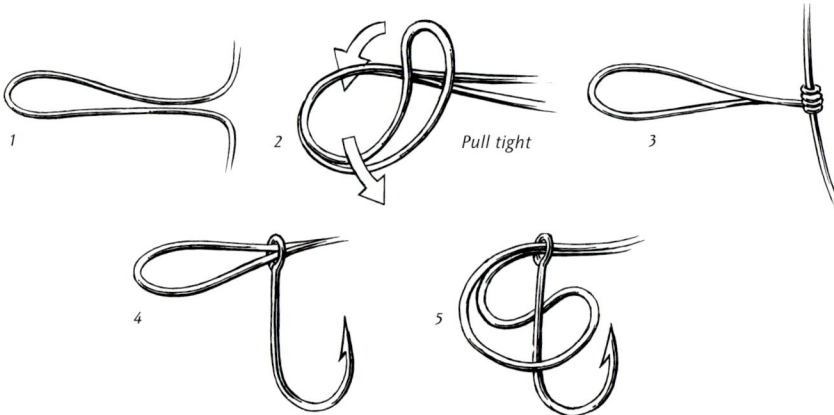

- Simple Clinch Knot – hook to nylon

- Improved Clinch Knot – for tying hook on

- Blood Knot – for joining two pieces of nylon together

Targeting the Species

Trout fishermen talk about presentation of the fly to the fish. Sea fishing also requires a deliberate presentation, and with most species a specific approach is often required. The detail may apply to the bait or type of food the species likes, or to the rig, tackle, or technique. Other tactical considerations are the habitat preferences of the individual species, and how this habitat is affected by the changing seasons.

HABITATS

Some species rove over a variety of habitats. Snapper, for example, are broad niche feeders, roaming widely from shallow mud flats, sandy bays, rocky reefs and deep water. Some species do not roam as far, but confine themselves to a particular habitat. Sandy bays, for example, are often home to red cod, gurnard, flounder and sole.

SEASONS

Snapper illustrate the seasonal factor – in summer in the Marlborough Sounds they may be found in very shallow water. I have caught them in water just a metre deep, and by moonlight in shallow mud flat areas I have seen snapper tails breaking the surface as they delve for pipis. After spawning in December they seem to temporarily disappear until mid-January, perhaps because the New Zealand coasts are busy with people at this time of year. A thinking angler adapts to that holiday water traffic by seeking out the more secluded bays. In winter, snapper tend to go deeper and again it is a matter of adapting by fishing in the 15 metres plus depths rather than shallow areas. Other species, such as red cod, are more commonly found inshore in winter.

TARGETING THE SPECIES

▲ *Red cod are usually more prevalent in winter months.*

In contrast, moki, especially larger breeding stock, tend to move out in winter for spawning. Kahawai and kingfish are similar, tending to move to deeper water and north during winter. Groper also have a seasonal pattern, but this differs between the north and the south.

It is important to understand the seasonal movements of the species you are targeting. The book on 'New Zealand Fishes' as listed in the Recommended Reading section will give you a good guide.

RIG

With regard to tackle rig, again it is a good idea to match this to the species you are seeking. To use snapper as an example again, this species is usually only taken with a running rig with the sinker at the end of the line. Sinker weight should be as light as possible – just heavy enough to keep the sinker on the bottom. Keep the sinker above the hook and a strong trace, or if there is no significant current, the best way of all is no sinker and just straylining. Such is the inborn wariness of the species that any unnatural weight when the snapper first picks up the bait will cause it to reject it. Snapper are also quick to detect unnatural resistance, so it is necessary to have the reel's drag set so lightly that the fish swims away with the bait and feels no resistance.

TARGETING THE SPECIES

BAIT

Some species are particular about the type of bait they will go for. Moki, for example, are rarely interested in fish bait, preferring crayfish and shellfish.

Other species will only be interested in live or moving bait. Two examples are kingfish and John Dory, both of which can be taken by jigging or with a live bait. Other species, such as the tarakihi, have small mouths that require small baits and smaller hooks.

HINT:
A strip can be cut from the flank or belly of a fish in a tapered shape. This looks like a small fish and may be tempting bait for larger species.

Then there are fish that are not fussy about bait type - snapper are feeders on a wide range of food from mussels and pipis to crabs and fish. Many anglers use pilchards to fish for snapper because they are easily obtained at bait stores. But it pays to think about where you are – if you are near a mussel farm for instance, a mussel tied onto the hook is a very logical bait to use.

Moki like this one have to be targeted with crayfish or mussel baits and are mostly caught at change of light. ▼

TARGETING THE SPECIES

UNEXPECTED CATCH

However prepared you are, remember that there are always exceptions to any rule in fishing. Even though you may target an individual species, be prepared for all sorts of surprises. If you target a relatively easy fish to catch, such as the blue cod, you may by chance catch tarakihi or kahawai as well.

On one occasion in a sandy bay by the Abel Tasman National Park I cleaned the cod and tarakihi we had caught and every so often tossed the fishy water from the bucket over the side. Beforehand I had cast out a light spinning outfit with small (size 12 trout hook) hooks and bait, thinking I might score a gurnard. I did score – but with half a dozen fine sole!

▼ *Mussel farms are always a good place to find snapper.*

TARGETING THE SPECIES

▲ *Kingfish are usually targeted by using a live bait, jigging or trolling.*

In summary, hooking the fish you want comes down to concentration and a focus on the habits and preferences of the species you hope to catch. This should determine the technique and tackle you use. The following pages will give you some general guidelines, but bear in mind that if you set out to target a particular species, you may catch some different fish along the way.

> **HINT:**
> *If the fish are not biting, experiment with a range of baits. It always pays to have more than one kind of bait, and squid is a reliable standby to always have on hand. It is a good idea to renew your bait every 15 to 20 minutes.*

Common species targeting guide

Barracouta

WHERE & WHEN: A member of the snake mackerel family, the barracouta is widespread around New Zealand, with larger numbers from Cook Strait southwards. Inhabits water from close inshore to depths of over 200 metres.

BAIT: Because of a varied diet ranging from krill to fishes, any bait from squid to fish to small fish will do. Will take a lure or jig readily.

RIG: Who would want to target barracouta? However, if you are after them for bait or perhaps smoking, then use a wire trace as their sharp teeth will usually sever nylon.

TIP: Barracouta do make reasonable bait, especially for groper.

Blue Cod

WHERE & WHEN: Bottom-dwellers, widespread but most abundant south from Cook Strait, ranging from shallow water to over 120 metres.

BAIT: Voracious feeders, any fish or squid bait or jig will take these bottom-dwelling fish.

RIG: Usually taken with a ledger rig and one or two long shanked 4/0 hooks on droppers.

TIP: Try a small jig (50g) or flasher rigs for a more sporting way.

Flounder

WHERE & WHEN: Often found in sandy bays and in estuaries up to tidal limit.

BAIT: Small shellfish baits or garden worms or finely cut squid.

RIG: Ledger rig, 2–3kg nylon with two droppers, and small (size 12 hooks) on light spinning tackle.

| TIP: | Ground bait with berley. If crabs are troublesome use tougher squid, for bait. |

Garfish

WHERE & WHEN:	Widespread. Often in shallow bays in spring and summer. Feeds on vegetable matter and small marine organisms.
BAIT:	Very small bait on very small hook. Slivers of fish flesh or skin, or even maggots!
RIG:	Light trout spinning outfit, size 14 hook on end with two or three split shot or a float with 15cm nylon between float and hook.
TIP:	Garfish will come in around a berley trail. If using split shot rig, move bait slowly through water. Garfish will take a small trout fly too. While good eating after being rolled with a milk bottle to crush bones, garfish are also a top snapper and kingfish bait.

Groper

| WHERE & WHEN: | Habits of North and South Island groper differ. Often known as hapuku in the north, the fish spawn in summer and come inshore in winter around deeper water reefs. In the South Island groper spawn in continental shelf depths in winter and move into coastal reefs in summer. |

BAIT:	Live baits such as "Jock Stewart" or "Maori Chief" sea perch are good - also large fillets of kahawai and barracouta.
RIG:	Set lines with heavy nylon (30kg plus) in deep water or rod and reel ledger rig with 40 kg and two 9/0 to14/0 hooks or a 250g metal jig.
TIP:	In deeper water use a non-stretch braided line such as "spider line" – the lack of elasticity allows the bite to be felt and the fish hooked.

Gurnard

WHERE & WHEN: Often found in sandy bays.

BAIT: Small bait, preferably shellfish such as mussels or pipis.

RIG: Light spinning-type tackle (3kg nylon) with small hooks and running rig.

TIP: Use small hooks and have hook point exposed, as gurnard have a habit of sucking baits. Set the hook instantly on a bite.

John Dory

WHERE & WHEN: Best in northern New Zealand around wharves and breakwaters.

BAIT: Live fish such as a small yellow-eyed mullet, spottie or very small kahawai.

RIG: 5-6kg line with a running rig and 10kg trace. Jigging is productive too.

TIP: Don't strike hard or aggressively. Play a john dory, as they have soft mouths.

Kahawai

WHERE & WHEN: Widespread but more abundant around and north of Cook Strait. Kahawai often move in surface schools but will range in mid-water and near bottom. Will ascend tidal rivers and lagoons, entering on rising tide. More abundant inshore in spring to autumn.

BAIT: Will take most fish or shellfish baits but baitfish such as pilchards and freshly caught yellow-eyed mullet are tops. Kahawai will readily take a metal lure, jig or saltwater fly.

RIG: For bait fishing use a running rig or a ledger rig. For tremendous sport, fish on light spinning tackle or fly fishing gear using a small metal lure or fly respectively.

TIP:	Kahawai can sometimes be selective, such as when homing in on whitebait in spring and early summer, then use light tackle and very small lure.

Kingfish

WHERE & WHEN:	Mainly summer and autumn, particularly around Cook Strait (generally most of the year in the north) and around reefs, rocks, underwater pinnacles and even man-made structures, especially where there is a tidal rip.
BAIT:	Live bait (e.g. small to medium-sized kahawai) or lures with jigging or trolling.
RIG:	10-15kg nylon with a "shock" trace 20-30kg. Jigging lures or trolling with Rapala-type or squid lures.
TIP:	Poppers that splutter the surface can be an exciting way to fish for "kingies" when they are surface feeding.

Moki

WHERE & WHEN:	Near shallow inshore reef areas, close in, perhaps 30 metres at most and even down to 10 metres, all year but best September to March.
BAIT:	Crayfish or shellfish, such as mussels or pipis. Fish baits rarely work on moki.
RIG:	6-8kg tackle with a 10-15kg trace on a running rig.
TIP:	Change of light (e.g. dawn or dusk) is the best time for most fish, but particularly so with moki.

Parore

WHERE & WHEN: Lives around shallow reefs and estuaries, mainly of northern New Zealand. Known as luderick in Australia, parore are vegetarian, feeding on weed.

BAIT: Eel grass or sea lettuce.

RIG: Long rod, 3kg nylon, a small float of "pencil" style and underneath a size 12 hook baited with weed and a few split shot on "trace."

TIP: Allow rig to drift in current. When a bite occurs wait for a count of ten before tightening to allow parore to suck bait in. Kill, gut and fillet parore immediately and they can be excellent eating.

Porae

WHERE & WHEN: Known as the morwong in Australia, the porae is most common along the north eastern coast, dwindling in numbers until Cook Strait. It inhabits mostly sandy areas near reefs, and lives on worms, shellfish and small invertebrates.

BAIT: Mussels and pipis are ideal, but fish baits, small in size, will take them.

RIG: A top sports fish, porae require strong tackle, about 6kg plus nylon and a ledger rig with droppers holding a 2/0 hook each.

TIP: The porae averages 2kg in size but is often bigger, and is sometimes confused with the tarakihi. Fish for porae on the sand adjacent to the reef, rather than on the reef itself, as porae have a distinct liking for the sand bottom from which they suck their food.

Red cod

WHERE & WHEN: Often found in sandy bays, usually in shallow water in winter.

BAIT: Red cod are not fussy so any bait (e.g. squid, fish) will do.

RIG: Ledger rig (sinker at bottom) with a dropper (or two) or running rig.

TIP: Gut red cod as soon as caught if you want them for the table. The flesh cooks to a white colour with a delicate texture.

Snapper

WHERE & WHEN: Roams widely, but generally shallower areas in summer and deeper waters in winter.

BAIT: Pilchards and freshly caught yellow-eyed mullet and garfish are best, but snapper enjoy a wide-ranging diet so mussels, squid, most fish fillets and even freshwater eel are also good.

RIG: Usually only taken with a running rig and trace rather than a ledger rig. Have the reel's drag set lightly for when fish picks up the bait and runs.

TIP: The weight of your sinker should be the minimum required for the tidal current. If you're fishing in still water or at "slack" water at high or low tide, try a strayline (i.e. no sinker).

Sole

WHERE & WHEN: In sandy bays.

BAIT: Small shellfish or squid.

RIG: Size 12 hook on light spinning tackle, ledger rig as for flounder, with light sinker (e.g. 3 or 4 split shot may suffice).

TIP:	Both sole and flounder will take a saltwater fly. Use a small weighted fly lure on a size 10 hook and scoot it in jerks across the bottom.

Tarakihi

WHERE & WHEN:	Widespread, tarakihi love "rough" ground anywhere from 5 to 50 metres in depth.
BAIT:	Tarakihi have small mouths, so small bait is best. Try kahawai, tuna or other filleted fish, or squid or mussel.
RIG:	Small hooks on 5kg line, or 8kg in deeper water where the bigger sub-species "king" tarakihi may be encountered.
TIP:	Tarakihi will sometimes just suck the bait rather than biting boldly. A sensitive rod tip will enable you to detect these soft bites.

Trevally

WHERE & WHEN:	Most abundant around North Island and down to Cook Strait to depths of 70 metres. Wide ranging in habitat from beaches to shallow harbours, surface schooling, near rocky reefs – you name it!
BAIT:	Any fresh fish, but shellfish such as mussels are best.
RIG:	This is an excellent fighting fish, so use nylon about 6-8kg breaking strain, with ledger rig on rod with "beef".
TIP:	Trevally have "soft" mouths so play them with firm care. A long-handled landing net is advisable for the final flurry at the boat or off rocks.

Trumpeter

WHERE & WHEN: Mainly South Island, but also caught on North Island's east coast off Hawke's Bay and Wairarapa. Best in early spring and summer in 30 to 90 metres of water.

BAIT: Cut fish bait on 8/0 hooks with 15-20kg tackle. Whole small squid is a top bait for trumpeter. Jigs which impart a fast action are good.

RIG: Use ledger rig and a fast action rod with power butt section.

TIP: If jigging in deeper water with nylon, compensate for stretch of line by giving half a dozen quick winds of the reel, then let jig flutter to bottom.

Fishing the Estuary

Estuaries are important places for sea fish, and great places for sea fishing. They can be a spawning ground for a number of species, as well as a feeding ground for juveniles that attract bigger fish. While fishing in estuaries I have caught not only kahawai, but snapper, trevally, red cod and john dory, and have seen kingfish smashing in amongst a shoal of kahawai.

Estuaries are fascinating areas, radically changing in water level and appearance every six hours as high and low tides interchange. Incoming tides bring yellow-eyed mullet and other baitfish into the river. A typical New Zealand river flows into a lagoon, which, due to wave action, frequently floods on the full tide.

KAHAWAI IN ESTUARIES

Kahawai are a prime species to target in estuaries, as they pursue baitfish and may swim two or three kilometres upriver. Incoming tides may offer good fishing, but beware — the dominant waves may dunk you and can be dangerous. I prefer an outgoing tide, usually an hour after full tide, as the outward river flow begins to assert itself, dulling the impact of the waves. There is another reason too, more to do with fishy matters. As the river begins to increase its flow, kahawai will hold in the flow or under it, waiting for any herrings to be swept down. It is not unlike a typical rapid in a river with quieter water near the bank.

Although the flow of the outgoing river may look swift, it is a deception of water hydraulics. In any channel, the current velocity is three times greater near the surface than near the bottom where there is a quiet layer. Fish such as kahawai have little trouble holding in this quiet zone while watching the faster water above. I tend to fish here using a spinner with a medium-speed retrieve. Many anglers fish the lure too quickly. Again, be

FISHING THE ESTUARY

flexible and vary your retrieve if strikes are not forthcoming. I have found on occasions that a spinner tossed upstream on a 45° angle and brought downstream will take kahawai when the usual 'cross and down' fails. On a few occasions I have found that a cast across and then hardly retrieving, just letting the current work the lure, can result in strikes. Kahawai are not always easy to catch. With polarised glasses aiding vision, I have seen big kahawai just following a lure without taking it. When I see this occurring I switch lures, perhaps going to a different colour or a smaller size.

Size can be an important factor at a time when kahawai are selectively feeding on smaller fish. I recall one morning at a Waikato west coast river mouth when it was whitebait season. I caught several big kahawai fishing with a light spinning outfit and using a very small, slim silver lure barely 3cm long to imitate the whitebait. There were numerous other anglers there using the usual kahawai spinners, 5-8cm long, but I only saw one other kahawai caught.

HINT:
If you encounter feeding kahawai there may be snapper underneath having an opportunistic feed from the scraps. Slowly lower a running rig with a yellow-eyed mullet bait down to the bottom. A fast moving lure, jinking in the light as it sinks, will probably be snapped up by the kahawai.

TARGETING OTHER SPECIES

Other species will enter estuaries too. Snapper can mooch up on the ingoing tide, and a running rig and small yellow-eyed mullet would be a logical tactic here. Even if a snapper is not caught, there is a good chance that kahawai, red cod, trevally or some other species might chance along.

One species that does need to be deliberately targeted is the flounder. Food for flounders comprises invertebrates, worms, small crabs and other food that they find in sand. Flounder range from depths of 50 metres up into estuaries and up rivers. The tackle for flounder should be: a trout spinning or similar light tackle outfit; a line with no more than 2kg breaking strain; a few split shot pinched onto the nylon; and a small hook about size 12 or 14. Garden worms or small pieces of shellfish such as mussel can be used for bait.

Surfcasting

Surfcasting is one of the most popular forms of sea fishing. In theory and with the aid of a long rod, you cast your baited hook out past the breaking waves to where feeding fish may be foraging. However, this technique requires a degree of observation and thought.

OBSERVATION

A keen sense of observation will give you a good angle on where to fish. It helps to observe the beach at low tide, preferably from a hill or sand dune, and to note the location of rock outcrops, channels and gutters where fish tend to congregate. You can also identify these areas by watching the surface of the sea. Waves break over shallow water but dissipate over deeper areas such as channels or holes. Then, as they reach the inner edge of a gutter, waves will build up again. Other things to look for are patches of darker coloured water, which indicate greater depths — polarised glasses are a great help. On the beach, look for the grouped empty shells of pipis and cockles as these are often evidence of a nearby shellfish bed.

Having observed the beach and channel structure at low tide, you have a few hours to wait until the tide moves in - time to anticipate that big catch!

THE GEAR

Surfcasters often use a rod about 3.5 metres long and usually with a fixed spool reel, which is sometimes referred to as an 'egg-beater.' On beaches such as Ninety Mile Beach in Northland, where the waves are high, a longer rod, perhaps 4 to 4.5 metres long, may be used because its extra length helps to keep the line above the waves.

SURFCASTING

Line of 5–6kg is ample. Far from being a disadvantage, this lighter line will allow lighter sinkers, yet longer casts, in order to reach an outlying channel. If a big fish is hooked on a long length of line, there is considerable elasticity – an insurance against a break-off.

Teardrop or spoon sinkers (also pyramid and hollow style) are usually used for surfcasting, but a ball sinker should be used with a running rig for snapper. Opt for smaller hooks such as 2/0 or 3/0 either in beak or kahl style. When using a lighter line it is advisable to use a trace of perhaps 10kg breaking strain, either as a half-metre running rig leader or as a 'shock' tippet with the ledger rig, connected to the main line by a swivel.

There are several advantages to using a lighter line:

- Casting is easier
- It is more sensitive to feeling 'soft' bites
- It is less likely to drag in the waves
- It can be cast further

> **HINT:**
> What rig to use? I personally opt for a running rig when surfcasting in most beach situations and where snapper are present. While a ledger rig will suit red cod, shark kahawai etc., a running rig is necessary to take snapper. Any time a school of snapper or a big solitary snapper may come along a running rig will increase your chances of hooking one or two.

Beach casting technique.

SURFCASTING

Use a beach spike to drive your rig into the sand. If needed, you can make a simple support from a length of PVC piping with one end tapered to drive into the sand.

SPECIES

Surfcasting has a delightful and unpredictable element as to the catch. Kahawai, snapper, gurnard, red cod, dogfish, and stingrays are all likely in sandy areas, while near rocks and kelp it is possible to catch blue moki using shellfish for bait. Consequently, baits can range from the durable squid to kahawai, yellow-eyed mullet, pilchards or shellfish.

> **HINT:**
> It's worthwhile having a few spinners with your surfcasting gear. If kahawai or kingfish show up, thrashing after baitfish close in, you can switch to the spinner.

TIMING

An incoming tide is probably the best phase to fish. Similarly, early morning or evening and into dusk are prime times as the light is not too bright. Calm, cloudy days will suit midday fishing on an incoming tide. An offshore breeze will mean calmer seas and more settled conditions, ideal for fish. If conditions encourage fish to come inshore and cruise the channels then your chances are immeasurably increased.

> **HINT:**
> Don't go too heavy or too light with sinkers when surfcasting. Use the biggest sinker that will keep your bait generally in one place – a small amount of movement is not a bad thing. Trial different sizes and find the best for the day.

Fishing from Rocks

Rocky shores, particularly those with kelp, are prime spots to fish for various species of all sizes. Small fish are attracted to this habitat because kelp provides cover. Larger fish, such as snapper and kingfish, will follow these smaller species – as long as they are not disturbed. A rocky coast often extends out into the sea, with offshore reefs also providing good fish habitat.

A current washing a rocky shore is always a good place to fish because it produces foaming water – an attractive habitat for fish. The aerated water is like a rapid in a river, swirling food around and providing cover for fish. Small fish such as pilchards and other baitfish will feed in this moving water, and kahawai, kingfish and snapper are likely to gather on the fringes.

PREPARATION

The best time for fishing varies from area to area. Some places have better fishing on the first half of a rising tide (low to half tide) while others are best on the second three-hour phase. It is a matter of getting to know your territory by experimenting and finding the best times to fish. Once you have identified the best tidal phase, the optimum time is for that to coincide with a change of light, such as early morning or evening.

To find a good location, observe the current flow. A rock jutting out into the current creates a flow around that rock and an eddy in the lee. An eddy is an ideal place to find baitfish because from there, they watch the current for food being carried along. These baitfish in turn attract the larger fish you may be after.

> **HINT:**
> White-water off rocks is always a good area to focus on. Large predators can lurk around white-water, concealed from baitfish, while other fish cruise the washed zone looking for dislodged food.

Another factor in determining your location or the time that you choose to fish may be access to a safe ledge - this may be covered at high tide.

EQUIPMENT

Casting long distances is not as crucial when fishing from the rocks as it may be when surfcasting from a beach. A rod should be medium to fast action, about 3 metres long, and with a fixed spool reel of the 'bait-runner' style. The line should be about 10kg heavier than for surfcasting as the territory is rougher and fish such as kingfish may be bigger. If you are targeting bigger fish, use a 5/0 hook. For snapper use a floating bait (i.e. no sinker) or a small sinker-running rig style, set immediately above the hook. A long-handled gaff or net is essential for most rock fishing situations.

BAIT

Because fish are relatively close in, berley should be used to attract baitfish, which in turn will bring the larger predators, your target species. Select a gutter in the rocks where the waves surge in and out, place the berley in a container, and let the outgoing waves suck the scent out into the sea. Handfuls of berley can also be thrown 5-10 metres out. Often baitfish such as garfish or yellow-eyed mullet can be hooked out from your berley trail by using a small threadline outfit and a size 12 hook with a tiny bait. This then provides you with totally fresh bait or live bait.

A good bait for snapper, kahawai, trevally or other predatory fish is a small baitfish or at least a frozen pilchard. Catch a kahawai and you have prime live bait to use for kingfish. It is good insurance to tie your rod and reel to a secured rope if live baiting. A large kingfish can take off with a rush! A dog clip attached to a stout cord or rope makes for easy unclipping. Live baits can be fished with or without a balloon. Balloons can be helpful at getting a live bait out when there is an offshore breeze.

FISHING FROM ROCKS

The balloon is attached with heavy cotton to a swivel where the line joins the heavier weight trace. This setup allows the balloon to come free when a kingfish strikes.

TACTICS

When a fish is hooked, the angler is limited in being able to play the fish. Basically you have to try to dictate the battle within the limit of your line's breaking strain. Keep your rod high and try to get the fish to come near the surface, away from rocks and kelp. It is very likely you will land fish, but inevitably you will get broken too. 'You win some, you lose some' certainly applies to rock fishing but all up, it can be an exciting sport and very productive for large fish.

> **HINT:**
> *It is amazing how effective side strain is in playing a fish. Similarly a hooked fish can often be steered in the direction you want by walking slowly back. You must be ready to release the pressure in case the fish makes a lunge, but chances are you'll 'walk' the fish to where you want.*

SAFETY

When fishing from rocks follow these safety rules:
- Wear non-slip footwear.
- Never fish alone.
- Before you take up a fishing position watch it for 5-10 minutes to note any abnormal waves that might rear up.
- Never turn your back on the sea.
- Keep alert!

Small Boat Fishing

I once owned both a 5 metre run-about boat powered by a 40hp outboard, and a 3 metre aluminium dinghy. When snapper fishing in the Marlborough Sounds I caught far more snapper from the aluminium dinghy. I still have the 'tinnie' (as aluminium boats are often called), and it often pays off with good catches. Sure, the sheltered nature of the Marlborough Sounds suits an aluminium dinghy, but aluminium boats that range in sizes from 3–5 metres are ideally suited to most inner coastal sea fishing, as long as safety requirements are met (see *Safety*).

HINT:
Birds such as gulls, terns and shearwaters are always on the lookout for feeding fish because they get to pick up some juicy scraps. So any birds fluttering around in the one spot are a clue that there are fish underneath.

▲ *Birds are a sign of feeding fish.*

SMALL BOAT FISHING

Safety

Small aluminium boats are not suitable in deep, turbulent water situations and particular care should be taken in the open sea. Small aluminium boats with no auxiliary motor can get into trouble if a strong offshore wind springs up and is allied with motor failure. Tinnies are light and can be quickly blown along by a strong wind. A boat must be adequately powered and have a backup in case of failure. It should also carry:

- *Lifejackets*
- *A set of oars*
- *A good anchor*
- *Safety flares*
- *A light if you fish into the night to give a visible warning to other boats*

Do not stand up to cast or to net or gaff a fish.

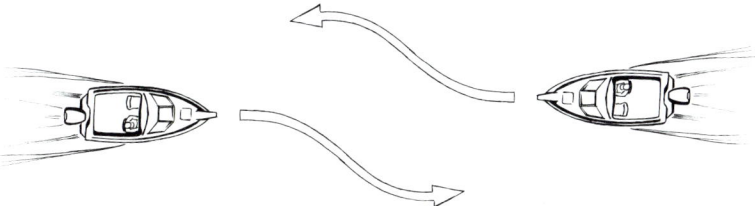

Boating 'rule of the road' - keep to the right when approaching another oncoming boat.

LOCATIONS

Mud and sand flats are ideally suited to small boat fishing. These tidal areas are great because they are rich in fish 'tucker' such as crabs, worms, eels, flounder and sprat-sized baitfish. On a rising tide bigger fish will come into an estuary to feed, sometimes in fairly shallow water. For example, snapper, which are normally very wary, will enter the shallows of sand flats from North Auckland to the Firth of Thames, Coromandel and a host of other tidal estuarine areas south to the Marlborough Sounds. Kahawai are also likely, and even kingfish.

SMALL BOAT FISHING

The shallow waters at the heads of inlets where a creek or stream enters also offer large fish an abundance of food from crabs to shellfish, and small fish to eels – it is that smorgasbord that entices prowling snapper into very clear water.

> ### *Equipment for catching snapper*
> *Snapper tackle for a mud flat is similar to that used for other snapper locations. A running rig is used with the hook at the bottom, as well as a trace of 10-20kg breaking strain nylon, a split ring or swivel, a sinker as light as the tidal currents will allow and preferably a round ball type. If the current is light, it is preferable to use no sinker. The rod should be light and sensitive in the tip but have strength in the butt and middle, and be about 2–2.2 metres in length. The reel can be a straight fixed spool or, better still, a lighter bait feeder model with about 200 metres of 4–6kg nylon.*

BAIT

Bait can range from squid – which is ideal if spotties are threatening to strip hooks clean – to pilchards, kahawai strips, mussel tied onto the hook, or freshwater eels. It is also good to try berley placed in a bucket with small holes in the bottom, or a berley container, hung over the side to let minute pieces of berley drift down current, enticing fish such as snapper towards the boat. An old mesh onion bag makes a good berley container too.

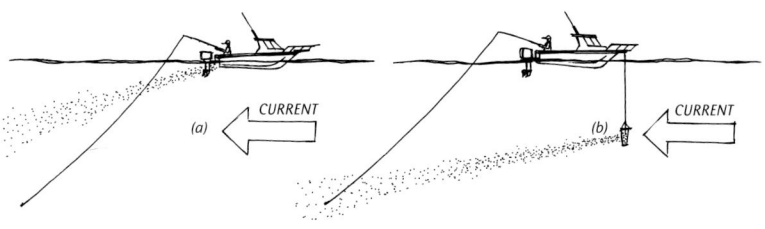

Proper berley use in deeper water – (a) wasted effort, (b) correct.

SMALL BOAT FISHING

Fresh bait is best of all, so it is worth taking a spinning rod along as you may chance upon a shoal of kahawai. Frequently in the berley trail yellow-eyed mullet (herring) and garfish will come in. These can be caught with a small hook and used for bait.

Take a bait board – a piece of timber about 3cm deep and 60 by 30cm in size, a knife, a plastic box with a lid (or a sack) to shield fish from the direct sun, and a landing net.

CHOOSING WHERE TO FISH

Some shallow tidal areas may be relatively featureless bays; others may be a network of side bays and side channels feeding into a main channel. Get to know the layout of channels and higher flats of the area you fish. This is best done at low tide, from a hillside, by cruising the channels in a dinghy, or by walking on the flats. If walking at low tide, look for telltale signs of snapper such as the round hollows where they have been excavating for shellfish. Note the location of shellfish beds that are likely to attract foraging snapper.

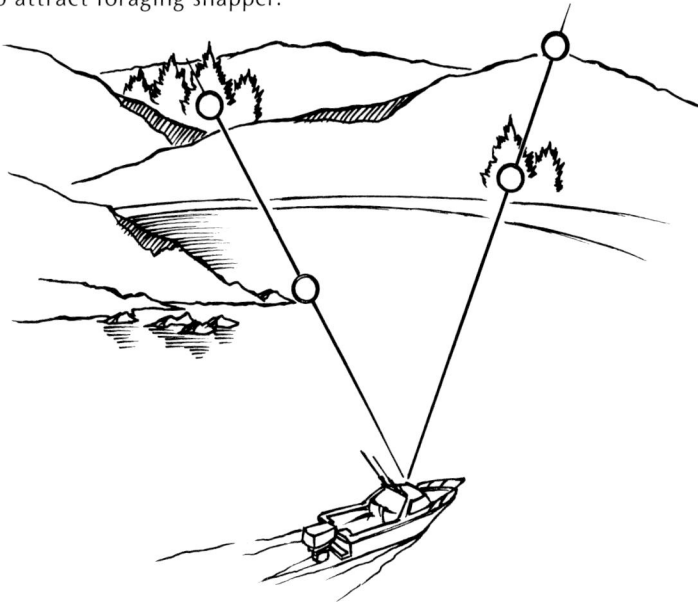

Using two lines of sight (two identifiable objects on each line) to relocate a good fishing spot.

SMALL BOAT FISHING

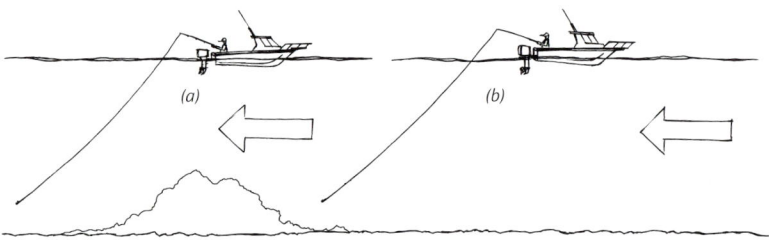

Positioning of the boat is important relative to current and a fishy spot such as a reef. Picture (a) shows a wasted effort; (b) is correct.

In a network of channels I often opt for a spot on the edge of the drop-off and at the convergence of two channels, rather than a spot up one channel. In a single channel situation, I like to fish at a drop-off, reasoning that fish will come up over the lip onto the shallower flats as the tide rises, or will prowl along the drop-off itself.

TIMING

A rising tide is a good time to fish – preferably one that peaks one to two hours after dark. For example, a high tide at 9pm with a sunset at 8pm or thereabouts would be an ideal combination of a flooding tide and the change of light. Similarly, early morning with a sunrise of 6am and a high tide of 8am is good. It is during the change of light from day to night, and then from night to day, that fish often feed strongly.

A falling tide on the first half of the ebb can also be productive. Some successful anglers claim it is superior to an incoming tide, but I prefer the incoming tide because the snapper coming in on that phase are likely to be hungrier.

On sand flats sea lice are rarely the problem they are in deeper water, so fishing into the night is possible. A bright moon is ideal and does not seem to scare snapper as it does

HINT:
If you see a school of surface feeding fish, cruise in and then cut the motor. Drift within casting range and then cast to the edge of the shoal with spinning gear. Going in too close with the motor will scatter the fish.

trout. It is at night that the bigger snapper are bolder and come onto sand flats to prey and forage.

TACTICS

The use of a dinghy enables stealth and finesse. Everything in shallow sand flat fishing, particularly for snapper, must be like 'tip-toeing on egg shells.' When getting the dinghy into place, it is a good idea to cut the motor a hundred metres away and quietly row into position. Any motor noise in shallow water will scare fish away. Once eased into position, drop the anchor quietly, set the berley trail and cast out well to the side of the dinghy, setting the drag to as light as possible. A snapper will pick up the bait and move off with it. Don't be too quick to tighten – let the snapper go 10 metres or so before setting the hook.

Stealth is especially important in shallow water. The sound of a rod bumping against the boat can be transmitted through water a surprising distance. Similarly, try not to drop a sinker. One good idea is to put a sack or old piece of carpet in the bottom of the boat to muffle any noises. Common-sense is needed in fishing from a small boat, especially an aluminium dinghy. Minimise movement in the dinghy by carefully packing equipment before you take to the water – you will enjoy the results of being well prepared.

> **HINT:**
> Barbless hooks have much merit. They allow the hook to be removed quickly which means you get your bait back into the water pronto and also allows for release of undersized fish or if practising "catch-and-release". Use a pair of suitable pliers to crush the barb of the hook. Barbless hooks do not mean more lost fish as long as pressure is maintained on a hooked fish.

Lure Fishing

Fishing with a lure is very effective, particularly on species such as kahawai, kingfish and tuna. For the shore angler, spinning can be great fun at river mouths (see *Fishing the Estuary*), and works well off rocky shorelines, and even off beaches when kahawai have been chasing baitfish close to the shore. Trolling a lure behind a boat is likely to score kahawai and kingfish, and perhaps skipjack tuna, albacore tuna and other surface feeding fish. Keep an eye out for birds – they are a good clue as to whether fish are feeding near the surface or not. If you find a school of feeding fish, do not take the boat through them. The disturbance upsets the fish and makes them disperse. Instead arc around the feeding fish so that your lure, perhaps 40-50 metres behind, passes through the feeding frenzy.

HINT:
Lures should not spin, otherwise the line will twist and kink causing tangles. Put a link swivel on the lure itself and a straight swivel less than a metre back where the trace of heavy breaking strain joins the main line.

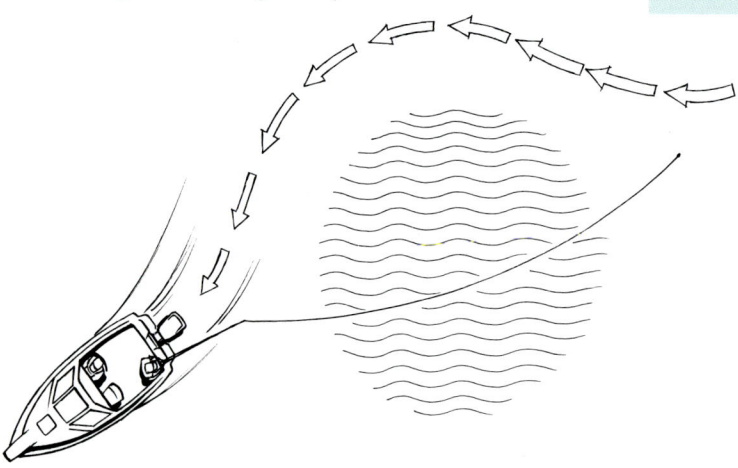

Trolling around a shoal of surface feeding fish so as not to disturb them while bringing the lure into their feeding zone.

CHOICE OF LURE

The lures to use depend on the target species. If you are trying to catch kahawai, use small lures about 5cm long; if kingfish are around use a bibbed lure of the Rapala type. A good idea to test the speed required is to troll your chosen lure on a few metres of line by the boat where you can observe its action. Generally, slim metal lures require a faster speed than more compact-shaped ones. Bibbed lures require just enough speed to make them wobble. A good general rule is to troll at low speeds - anglers commonly troll too fast.

Trolling lures come in various styles including traditional metal sliced chrome (kahawai) lures, stingsilda, diving fish-shaped lures, plastic squids, skirted lures, surface poppers and bibbed lures.

JIGGING

A newer form of lure fishing is jigging. It rose to popularity in the late 1980s and is basically a vertical form of spinning. Rather than cast the lure out and retrieve it, the lure is dropped over the side of a boat and left to sink to the bottom. The rod is then raised and lowered just a few metres.

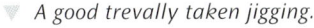
A good trevally taken jigging.

LURE FISHING

Tackle for this approach is specialised - a 2–2.5 metre long rod with a fast action, a sensitive tip, and power in the butt. Fixed spool, otherwise known as egg beater or threadline reels, can be used. Particularly common are the bait feeder type used on fighting drag, but the best are overhead (star drag) reels. Nylon weights may range from 4–20kg, depending on the species being targeted.

Jig lures may range from conventional metal lures and soft plastics to compact, heavier spoons and high-speed deeper water jigs suited to kingfish. The weight and style of jig lure will relate to the species, the depth of the water, and the current. However, use the smallest lure that you can get to the bottom. A rule of thumb is to simply add a zero to your line weight. A 4kg line suits a 40g lure, 8kg an 80g lure, 10kg a 100g lure and so on. There is a tolerance to this rule of thumb of about plus or minus 20–25 percent. Jigs are usually sold with treble hooks but I suggest you replace the treble with a single hook.

Jigging can be done from an anchored boat or by drifting. The latter allows coverage of a variety of bottom feeders, but it does increase the chances of snagging. Nevertheless the drift jigging technique is looked upon by most anglers as superior to jigging from an anchored boat.

The basic jigging technique involves opening the bail arm on your fixed spool reel or free spooling the overhead reel so the lure sinks. Sometimes fish will grab the lure as it seesaws its way down. Strike immediately by turning the fixed spool reel handle to flick the bail arm over, or flipping the overhead reel into gear.

> *The American fishing writer Ed Zern once wrote, 'Fishermen are born honest but they soon get over it.' So don't believe all the tales you hear. Some anglers forget their blank days and may give the impression you're a failure for having them.*

HINT:
A falling barometer usually indicates a bad time to fish, whereas a rising one means good fishing. Flat seas and bright sunlight are usually too clear. A light chop or joggle on the sea is best.

LURE FISHING

Once the lure has reached the bottom, put the reel into gear and raise the rod tip from the sea surface to above your head, probably 2-3 metres, then let the lure drop to the bottom. A variation is to keep your rod tip pointed towards the water, flick the reel into gear and retrieve it at least several metres straight up, and then let it fall to the bottom again.

Speed jigging is a technique used on species like kingfish and tuna where the rod tip is kept down and the lure reeled as fast as possible. A good idea is to use a heavy shock trace a metre in length, with a swivel as the link from trace to line. The 'clunk' of the swivel as it comes through the tip ring warns the lure is not far behind!

Saltwater Fly-fishing

Saltwater fly-fishing has been around for years in the USA and in recent decades has spread to Australia and now New Zealand. It seems destined to consolidate itself and become a saltwater sport fishing method in its own right. Saltwater fly-fishing guru Sam Mossman says the method fits in with his attitude to fishing – 'more fun from fewer fish' – and that 'saltwater fly-fishing is the most fun way to fish that I know.'

The potential for variety in saltwater fly-fishing is immense. Sam Mossman for example, has battled with and taken over two dozen species on the fly rod. Among them are kahawai, kingfish, trevally, blue maomao, snapper, john dory, various species of shark, skipjack tuna, tarakihi, blue cod, trumpeter, flounder, gurnard, yellow fin tuna, and – incredibly – groper in Fiordland.

SPECIES

The kahawai is undoubtedly the number one species for the budding saltwater fly-fisher to target. Any river mouth may offer high chances of hooking a kahawai, and any shoals of kahawai working the surface will usually take a fly flicked to them.

EQUIPMENT

While trout fly-fishing gear can be used, saltwater situations such as fishing from a jetty, boat, rocks or from a river mouth, can cause havoc to gear unless it is immediately stripped, cleaned and washed with hot water each time after use. It is better to use specialised saltwater fly-fishing gear, which New Zealand companies such as Kilwell now produce,

◁ *The author with a kahawai taken on the fly rod. Saltwater fly-fishing, a rage overseas, seems destined for the same popularity in New Zealand over the next decade.*

SALTWATER FLY-FISHING

although quality equipment is relatively expensive.

Fly rods are designed to handle a certain weight of line. In saltwater fly rods, the line weight may be anywhere from 8-12kg or more. The ideal saltwater fly rod should have 'beef' or power in the butt section. For fishing saltwater flats or river mouths, the following is suggested:

- Rod: Fast action 8 weight
- Reel: Large arbor saltwater reel
- Line: Weight 8 with wet tip and/or sinking
- Flies: Clouser Minnow, Crazy Charlie, Lefty's Deceiver, Surf Candy are some of the better known fly patterns
- Other useful equipment – polarised dark glasses, a wide brim hat, and a casting basket strapped around the waist to contain line.

Remember in saltwater fly-fishing that the old KISS formula – Keep It Simple Stupid – is particularly relevant. Only half a dozen flies are needed, and the less gear you have the less there is to lug around and for your line to get caught on.

LOCATION AND TIMING

Likely areas to try saltwater fly-fishing are estuaries and river mouths, sheltered bays, inlets and rocky coastlines. Wharves and jetties can be good for kahawai, small snapper and even species such as spotties, john dory and yellow-eyed mullet. Some fishers choose an incoming tide because fish will move up over flats. However, if you are fly-fishing, a falling tide means you have less

▲ *Yellow is a favoured colour in saltwater flies.*

SALTWATER FLY-FISHING

▲ *Saltwater fly-fishing adds a new dimension to sea fishing.*

water in which to search for fish. As outlined in the chapter on estuary fishing, kahawai on the outgoing tide can lie closer to the edge and are thus easier to reach with the fly rod.

TECHNIQUE

A cast of around 6 metres may be ample for kahawai close in, other times a 20 to 30 metre cast may be required. The line is retrieved into your casting basket and your retrieve should vary to suit the species. For example, for kahawai, strip the line in fairly quickly, but for gurnard, a slow, twitching, deep retrieve near the bottom is required.

In summary, the fly is frequently more appealing than a conventional metal lure to fish such as kahawai. It is more lifelike in shape and the feathers give a strong hint of realistic life. I have found that as long as fish are within reach of a fly rod cast, the fly will invariably out-fish spinners. Try learning to use a saltwater fly-fishing rod on the humble kahawai and then graduate to other species. While you do so, read Sam Mossman's definitive work, *Saltwater Fly-fishing in New Zealand*. You will be well and truly hooked!

Keeping a Diary

Keeping a diary on fishing trips has much merit. If you get enough data together, you will probably begin to see patterns emerging. For instance, on one snapper fishing trip in the Pelorus Sound, my friend and I moved several times throughout the day with little luck, until suddenly at about 4 o'clock it was as though somebody down below had thrown a switch. The snapper began to hit and the ensuing sport was fast and frantic. In seven hours we had caught nothing and then in a couple of hours we had all the snapper we could wish for. Why? Was it the falling tide rather than a rising tide, or was it the magical 'bite time', or perhaps it was just the particular place on that phase of the tide? Collecting data on a day like that can give some interesting information for analysis and a strong lead for tactics on future trips.

Photocopy the page opposite and you will be able to keep an accurate record of all your future sea fishing expeditions.

BITE TIME

The main bite time can be calculated by when the moon is directly overhead, i.e. halfway between the time of the rising of the moon and the time of the setting of the moon. These times can be obtained from the weather page in the daily newspaper. The secondary bite time is 12 hours different from the main bite time, i.e. when the moon is directly 'underneath.'

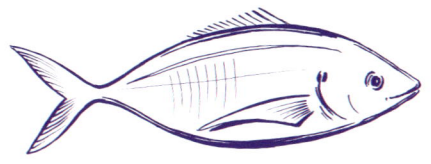

FISHING DIARY

DATE:

LOCATION:

TIME FISHED:

TIME FISH CAUGHT:

TIDE:

BITE TIME:

PHASE OF MOON:

FISH CAUGHT:

SUCCESSFUL BAIT:

FISH / WEIGHT:

COMMENTS:

The Last Cast – Conservation

The sporting philosophy you adopt for fishing is very much your choice, given that there are regulations as to bag limits, size limits, and other rules to be adhered to. I recommend that you aim to limit your kill, rather than kill your limit, and that releasing fish should be done as quickly and gently as possible.

Overstressed fish die, so it is a good idea to keep handling to a minimum. Barbless hooks are sometimes used by trout anglers practising catch and release and these can be used in sea fishing also. As long as pressure is kept on the line, the hook is unlikely to fall from its hold. With a pair of pliers, crimp the barb down. Similarly, single hooks are preferable to the treble hooks on many lures.

Hopefully this book has made you aware of the potential to go fishing and catch yourself a feed, and in doing so have a great time. Further your study and your awareness by reading more – I have recommended some further reading on pages 60–61. But remember the point from early in this book that 'the true function of an authority (writer) is to stimulate, not to paralyse original thinking.' Be a thinking angler, observant, analytical and experimental, and you'll find a fascinating world in saltwater sport fishing.

HINT:
When releasing a fish, a wet towel aboard the boat makes the job of catch and release so much easier. The fish can be held easily while the wet towel minimises any possible damage. Some trout anglers hold a fish upside down when removing the hook as they believe the fish will not struggle.

◄ *A good sized snapper – fresh from the Marlborough Sounds.*

Recommended Reading

Serious About Sportfishing by Sam Mossman, published by David Bateman, 1993. This is a comprehensive saltwater fishing guide, detailing advances in technique and tackle and covering in depth all methods.

Saltwater Fly-fishing in New Zealand by Sam Mossman, published by David Bateman, 2000. This is an essential, detailed guide to this exciting and challenging style of saltwater fishing.

The Kiwi Catch by Sam Mossman, published by Reed Publishing, 1998. The author targets 15 fish species from the kahawai and blue cod to kingfish and snapper, tarakihi, trevally, groper and several others.

All About New Zealand's Favourite Fish by Steve Snedden and Gary Kemsley, published by Halcyon Press, 1996. This is a book that emphasises targeting the species and gives detailed advice on how to approach each.

Fishing Smarter by Tony Bishop, published by Halcyon Press, 1997. This book basically aims to make you one of those 10 percent of anglers who catch 90 percent of fish.

Daryl Crimp's Guide to Sea Fishing in New Zealand published by Reed Publishing, 2002. This is a comprehensive guide to the intricacies and strategies of targeting the more popular fish species.

Hook, Line and Sinker by Daryl Crimp, published by Harper Collins, 2003. The how, why and where of catching 60 species of saltwater fish.

The Complete New Zealand Fisherman by Geoff Thomas, published by David Bateman, 1997. This has a comprehensive saltwater fishing section.

New Zealand Fishes by Larry Paul, published by Reed Publishing, 1986. This was reprinted in 2000, and has excellent identification of fish, and details on distribution and habits.

Hook Up on Kingfish by Mark Kitteridge, published by Reed Publishing, 2001. Everyone should catch a kingfish and this is the book to help you.

Seasons of Seafood by Daryl Crimp, published by Halcyon Press, 2001. This book features simple and delicious seafood recipes.

Glossary

Action (of a lure) – the particular movement of a lure that appears lifelike to the fish.

Artificial lure – a lure made of metal, plastic, wood or other material. An artificial lure usually imitates a small fish.

Backlash – an over-run of line on the reel when the line comes off quicker than the reel is revolving. Usually occurs with 'bait caster' type reels.

Berley – a mixture of fine fragments of fish, meat, bread, mash or perhaps fish oil that is put into the water to attract fish to the area of the baited hook.

Bird's Nest – a tangle of nylon often associated with fixed spool (spinning) reels.

Bite Time – the theoretical time (based on moon's zenith) when fish bite best. (See page 56.)

Breaking Strain – the theoretical limit at which a line will snap. So in theory a 5kg strain will snap when a 5kg weight is suspended. In practice it doesn't quite work like that. The 'bend' of the rod will absorb some strain so it's possible to land a much bigger fish than the breaking strain of the line.

Drag – an adjustment on the reel that acts as a brake when the fish is pulling.

Foul ground – a term to describe the rocky or stony area of the seabed.

Gimbal – a cup attached to a belt that allows the butt of the rod to be placed while fighting a fish. Usually associated with big game fishing or species like kingfish.

Gut (Gutter) – a depression or gutter in the seabed and in fishing, usually relating to a depression running underwater just off a beach.

Krill – minute, floating shrimp/plankton creatures on which fish feed.

Lateral line – the in-built radar of fish that contains sensitive nerves and runs along the flank.

Leader – sometimes called a trace, which in saltwater fishing is usually a length of heavier nylon which may be anywhere from 30-100cm or more long and which connects the main line to the hook.

Pelagic (fish) – fish that feed on or near the surface or in mid-water, e.g. kahawai, kingfish, trevally.

Popper – a floating lure that creates a wake with gurgling vibrations and attracts pelagic species.
Pumping (a fish) – the act of raising the rod and then lowering it while simultaneously winding, in order to retrieve line back onto the reel and to bring the fish closer.
Rig – a term used to describe the sinker/trace/hook combination.
Rod Action – where the rod bends when tension (by a fish) is applied to the line.
Rod Power (also 'grunt', 'beef') – the ability or strength of the rod to handle a usually powerful fish.
Run – the movement away (from the angler) by a fish when hooked.
Running Rig – where the line is free to pass through the hole of a sinker as the fish runs.
Side Strain – putting the rod to the side and parallel to the ground when a fish is hooked.
Sinker – shaped lead attached to line, to provide weight for casting the baited hook out.
Slack water – just before or after high or low tide when there is little or no tidal flow.
Sounding – a vertical run by a fish towards the seabed.
Spinner – metal lure that revolves or wiggles when retrieved and imitates a baitfish.
Split shot – very small lead pellets that are half-cut and which are squeezed onto nylon to give weight for casting.
Star Drag – type of reel (akin to bait caster).
Strayline – a baited hook and line with no sinker.
Strike – the raising of the rod to tighten the hook into a fish's mouth.
Strike – a 'bite' usually associated with spinning or trolling when a fish grabs the lure.
Tackle – the outfit of rod, reel, line and hook (or lure), sinker, etc.
Terminal tackle – the hook end of tackle comprising sinker, leader, hook, swivel, etc.
Ticer – particular type of metal lure.
Tinnie – aluminium boat, usually of dinghy size.
Trace – refer *Leader*.

How to Fillet a Fish

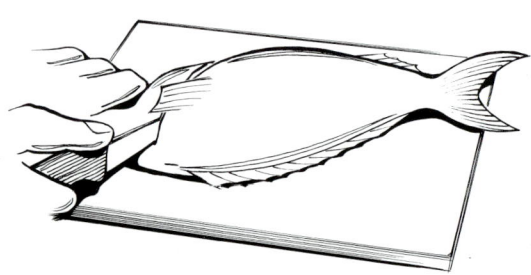

First gut the fish, then, holding the fish flat, make a cut directly behind the front dorsal fin.

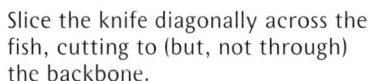

Slice the knife diagonally across the fish, cutting to (but, not through) the backbone.

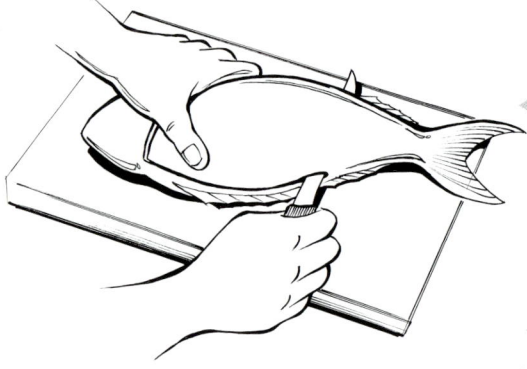

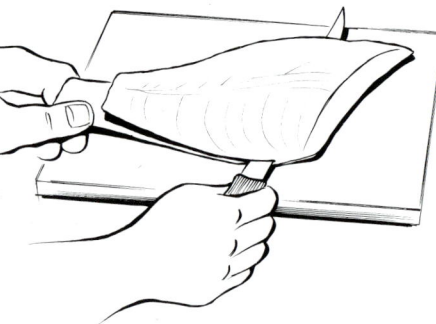

Run knife along and against the backbone. Keeping knife against ribs, cut flesh (fillet) away.

To remove the skin run a knife between the skin and flesh.